The Underwater Mystery

The Underwater Mystery

A Young Oceanographer's Introduction to Internal Waves

JIN TAN

XENO

Book design by Mark E. Cull

ISBN 978-1-939096-29-6 (Tradepaper)
ISBN 978-1-939096-69-2 (ebook)
ISBN 978-1-939096-30-2 (Library Binding)

The National Endowment for the Arts, the Los Angeles County Arts Commission,
the Ahmanson Foundation, the Dwight Stuart Youth Fund, the Max Factor Fami-
ly Foundation, the Pasadena Tournament of Roses Foundation, the Pasadena Arts
& Culture Commission and the City of Pasadena Cultural Affairs Division, the
City of Los Angeles Department of Cultural Affairs, the Audrey & Sydney Irmas
Charitable Foundation, the Meta & George Rosenberg Foundation, the Albert and
Elaine Borchard Foundation, the Adams Family Foundation, Amazon Literary
Partnership, the Sam Francis Foundation, and the Mara W. Breech Foundation
partially support Red Hen Press.

First Edition
Published by Red Hen Press / Xeno Books
www.redhen.org

For my parents and brother

Contents

The Underwater Mystery

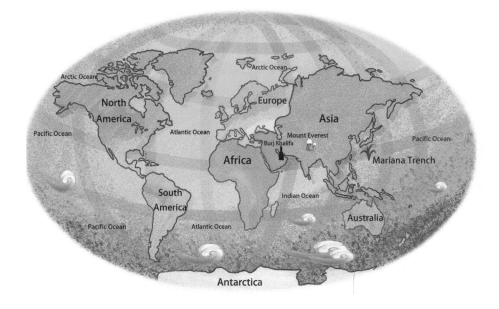

SECTION 1

Oceanography

Do you know . . .

Over **70%** of the surface of our planet is covered by ocean;

The ocean holds around **97%** of Earth's water;

Its surface area is around **360 million** square kilometers;

- this is more than **34** times the size of Europe, or around **14 and a half** times the size of North America.

On average, its depth is **3,682** meters.

- **4.5** times the height of Burj Khalifa, the tallest building in the world

The deepest part of the ocean, the Mariana Trench, is approximately 11 kilometers deep, about the height of more than **13** Burj Khalifas and even higher than **Mount Everest**.

The people studying and exploring the ocean are called **Oceanographers**, and the study of the ocean is called **Oceanography**.

Oceanography covers many topics, including the fantastic animals that live underwater, how ocean water moves around the world, why the ground beneath the sea changes, and the properties of the ocean. As you might have already noticed, oceanography involves a combination of many subjects, such as physics, chemistry, biology, geology, and engineering.

A very brief history

The formal study of the ocean began about 150 years ago when a group of scientists went on an expedition called *the H.M.S. Challenger* Expedition to collect data about the marine environment. They studied ocean temperatures, currents, marine life, and seafloor geology.

Modern oceanography started after World War II, when the U.S. Navy wanted to improve communication across the Atlantic and the use of submarines in war. Thanks to technology, oceanography quickly developed in the next few decades. Oceanographers now use a range of vehicles, devices, and even spacecraft to study the ocean.

Facts about the ocean

More than half of the oxygen we breathe comes from the ocean. You've probably heard of this somewhere: plants use photosynthesis to produce oxygen and sugar from sunshine, carbon dioxide, and water. The plants living in the ocean that are responsible for this massive oxygen production are called phytoplankton, a type of oceanic plankton.

The Challenger Deep in Mariana Trench is the deepest point on Earth's seafloor. Only two brave teams of people have ever made it down there in a submarine! On January 23, 1960, Jacques Piccard and Don Walsh dove into the Trieste and spent nearly five hours reaching the bottom. Then, more recently, on March 26, 2012, James Cameron went down in the Deepsea Challenger, spending only about two-and-a-half hours to reach the deepest point on Earth.

Submarines are pretty tight spaces. There are only a handful of spots inside a submarine where you could stretch out your arms and spin around without bumping into something—Cameron would be the envy of Piccard and Walsh!

Q: *Since oceanography is the study of the ocean, I'm guessing the study of internal waves in the ocean must be a branch of it?*

A: Very correct. To be more specific, internal waves are in the division of physical oceanography, which is the study of the physics in the ocean.

Internal waves

Physical oceanographers study many fascinating ocean phenomena, such as ocean circulation, tides, tsunamis, wind waves, etc. In this book, we will dive into internal waves. From the name, it's not hard to tell that they're a type of wave, probably in the ocean, as this book is definitely about oceanography. But before we go into any details of internal waves, let's hear a bit about an explorer's adventure.

Dead-water Phenomenon

Norwegian explorer Dr Fridtjof Nansen encountered the dead-water phenomenon in August 1893 while on board Fram on the Norwegian North Polar Expedition. This is the first time the phenomenon has been described.

Nansen's Diary
Kara Sea, Russia

> . . . When caught in dead water Fram appeared to be held back, as if by some mysterious force, and she did not always answer the helm. In calm weather, with a light cargo, Fram was capable of 6 to 7 knots (11.1 to 13.0 km/h). When in dead water she was unable to make 1.5 knots (2.8 km/h). We made loops in our course, turned sometimes right around, tried all sorts of antics to get clear of it, but to very little purpose . . .

He observed that dead water happened "where a layer of fresh water rests upon the salt water of the sea." But people had no idea what the mysterious force was at that time. We know that Fram met a wave, but it is not a wave you can always easily see at the ocean's surface. That's what confused Nansen and his team. It was an internal wave.

What are internal waves?

First, what is a wave? A wave is an oscillation that travels through matter and space. Energy is carried and transferred from place to place during this process. Sound is a wave, and sound energy is transferred when we hear a sound. Light is also a kind of wave. The heat we feel from the sun is an example of energy transfer. When it comes to oceanography, there are two critical waves in the ocean water column according to their position: surface waves and internal waves.

Imagine you are at the beach. When you've just finished building your sandcastle, a wave comes, trying to wash away your castle. That is a surface wave that travels between water and air.

> Q: *That sounds like all ocean waves. Where else can waves travel? In the ocean?*

> A: Exactly. Internal waves are between layers of water that have different densities. What is density, then? Density is the ratio of mass to volume. An object with a higher density is heavier than one with a lower density when they have the same volume.

Some oceanographers describe internal waves like this:
"Internal waves usually occur when there is stratification."

"Stratification" is a big word, but no worries, it has a simple meaning. Stratification in the ocean means that the ocean water is separated into different horizontal layers by density. Warmer and less salty water with a lower density is closer to the surface, whereas colder and more salty water with a higher density is closer to the bottom. Sun shines on the ocean's surface, heating water at the surface. As a result, the water closer to the surface tends to have a higher temperature than that deeper in the ocean. Therefore, a temperature variation is happening vertically within the water body. There is a salinity variation as well. Salinity is the saltiness of water, i.e., the amount of salt dissolved in the water. When the surface water evaporates, it leaves salt behind, making it saltier. Denser fluid (the general name for liquid and gas) sinks to the deeper layer because it is heavier. Hence, the salinity and density increase with depth. So, this sentence talks about the same thing but sounds like some highly complex science.

You might think: "But I don't see or feel any stratification at the beach. When I step into the water, there're no layers." This is because the stratification is less sharp than you might have imagined. Most of the time, there isn't a sudden rise of density within water. Internal waves don't always need super strong and distinct layers of different densities to form as long as some layering and disturbance occur. The stratification could be so gradual and gentle that you wouldn't notice, and the waves still can exist. When an internal wave passes by, this stratification is preserved. The wave will travel between the two layers, and the layers will not mix.

Now recall Nansen's story: the ship Fram encountered an internal wave. If there was an internal wave, there must have been stratification. But how? Remember that he was on an expedition to the North Pole. The melting sea ice provided fresh water at the ocean surface. Therefore, the water at the surface was less salty and had a lower density, while the water below was still very salty and dense. There was then an interface between the two layers of water. An internal wave was formed at the interface, which took away some of the ship's energy, which was supposed to be used to move it forward.

More about internal waves

Internal waves are commonly found across various bodies of water and even in the atmosphere. You can find them in:

coastal seas
straits
fjords
continental shelves
lakes

and even in the boundary layer of the atmosphere.

They are often found near sudden changes in the underwater landscape, like strait sills, continental slopes, and sandbanks.

Q: *How big can an internal wave be? How fast can it be?*

A: To answer these questions, we must first examine the properties of waves. A few wave properties that often attract scientists are crest, trough, amplitude, wavelength, frequency, and period. These sound like a lot, but they are straightforward to learn.

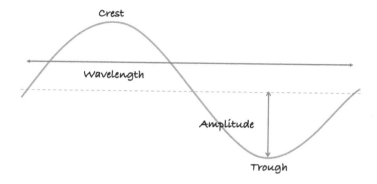

This drawing shows that the crest and trough are the highest and lowest points on the wave within a cycle, respectively. Amplitude is the maximum disturbance a wave creates. In other words, it is the maximum displacement of a point on the wave from the equilibrium position, or the rest position called by some, indicated by the horizontal line. You can find it by measuring the distance between a crest or trough and the horizontal line. Wavelength, on the other hand, is the distance between adjacent crests or troughs of the wave. Note that oceanographers look at a particular wavelength modification, such as half wave width. Half wave width, or half width for short, is half the width of a wave blob at half of its maximum amplitude. It is proposed as an essential parameter of a particular type of internal wave, internal solitary wave, which, according to the definition of wavelength, cannot be said to have a wavelength. Frequency, different from amplitude and wavelength, is the number of waves that pass by a point every second. People often use Hertz (Hz) as unit. 1 Hz is one cycle per second. Period is the opposite. It is the time taken for a wave to pass by a point.

As density differences between internal layers in the ocean are much more minor than between air and water, the gravitational restoring force—the force that brings a body to its equilibrium position—is much weaker. These internal waves can easily have dimensions greatly exceeding surface waves, while their time evolution and propagation are much slower. The maximum amplitude of the internal wave ever measured is around 200 meters, about the height of 2 Big Bens in London. Typically, the wavelength of an internal wave in the ocean varies from hundreds of meters to tens of kilometers. And periods can range from minutes to hours.

The formation of internal waves involves some energy supply. For an internal wave to be produced at the interface between two layers of water, energy must be applied to disrupt the equilibrium of the water. In other words, there must be disturbances that cause the vibration.

For scientists trying to explain Nansen's experience, discovering this is the final piece of the jigsaw. Stratification allowed an internal wave to form. However, what triggered the internal wave was the energy supplied by the ship Fram, the energy from the propulsion system. From this perspective, it sounds surprising that the boat was "held back" by some "mysterious force," and it was the ship itself which caused the force.

In nature, there are several ways of forming an internal wave. We'll look at three of the most common ones. All these movements (wind, tide, and fluid) provide energy, which triggers internal waves.

1. **Wind:** When the wind kicks up, it can stir the ocean's surface, creating severe turbulence that leads to internal waves.
2. **Tidal movement:** When interacting with underwater features like continental shelves and seafloor ridges, they can generate powerful internal waves.
3. **Fluid movement:** Warm and cold water currents sloshing around can cause severe turbulence, resulting in internal waves.

Do the word search below to test your familiarity with internal waves vocabulary! The answer is on the next page.

Internal Waves Vocabulary

TIDE
DISTURBANCE
UNDERWATER
WIND
RIDGE
DENSITY
LAKE
INTERNAL WAVE
STRAIT
DEAD WATER
LAYER
STRATIFICATION
FRAM
CURRENT
OCEAN
FJORD

N	O	I	T	A	C	I	F	I	T	A	R	T	S
E	T	D	N	B	D	R	E	D	D	U	O	N	D
V	A	E	D	R	W	S	R	L	E	R	V	L	R
A	D	N	N	D	T	T	T	A	A	L	S	Y	T
W	G	S	I	R	T	R	T	K	D	M	A	R	F
L	O	I	W	R	N	A	N	E	W	E	G	C	S
A	A	T	E	E	A	I	E	A	A	T	I	F	A
N	S	Y	G	Y	E	T	R	D	T	L	I	N	M
R	F	R	D	A	C	T	R	E	E	A	S	D	S
E	F	F	I	L	O	R	U	E	R	D	D	A	E
T	D	A	R	E	G	I	C	F	J	O	R	D	V
N	D	U	N	D	E	R	W	A	T	E	R	R	W
I	E	C	N	A	B	R	U	T	S	I	D	A	T
E	O	W	A	R	R	C	C	U	O	T	T	A	D

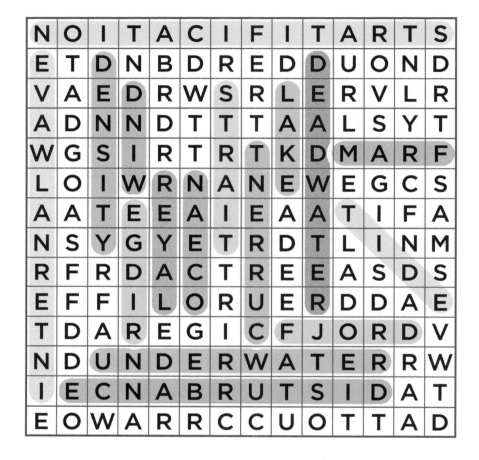

N	O	I	T	A	C	I	F	I	T	A	R	T	S
E	T	D	N	B	D	R	E	D	D	U	O	N	D
V	A	E	D	R	W	S	R	L	E	R	V	L	R
A	D	N	N	D	T	T	T	A	A	L	S	Y	T
W	G	S	I	R	T	R	T	K	D	M	A	R	F
L	O	I	W	R	N	A	N	E	W	E	G	C	S
A	A	T	E	E	A	I	E	A	A	T	I	F	A
N	S	Y	G	Y	E	T	R	D	T	L	I	N	M
R	F	R	D	A	C	T	R	E	E	A	S	D	S
E	F	F	I	L	O	R	U	E	R	D	D	A	E
T	D	A	R	E	G	I	C	F	J	O	R	D	V
N	D	U	N	D	E	R	W	A	T	E	R	R	W
I	E	C	N	A	B	R	U	T	S	I	D	A	T
E	O	W	A	R	R	C	C	U	O	T	T	A	D

Answers to Internal Waves Vocabulary Puzzle on page 21

SECTION 3

Generate an Internal Wave at Home

Now that you have acquired the basic knowledge of internal waves. You can use this knowledge to make an internal wave yourself. Create stratification within a water column and then produce a disturbance. It is as easy as it sounds.

All you need:

- food coloring
- water
- salt
- a piece of board (or any other flat, water-proof thing you can find at home that won't make your parents angry) that has a length of the inner width of the container
- a dropper (remember to clean it before using)
- a teaspoon to add salt
- a transparent rectangular container (not a too flat one)—ideally a water tank—with water filled up to half its height

A bit of math before you begin . . .

i. You will need to prepare salt water for this experiment. It is important to calculate the amount of salt you need precisely if you have noticed that it is not specified above. We want the salt water to have a density

~ 23 ~

of around 1.05 *g/cm³*. Therefore, according to the density formula, $density = \frac{mass}{volume}$, we can play around with the equation using the volume and mass of the water you filled in the water tank.

ii. The volume can be found using *volume = length × width × height*, or half the volume of the container, which you might find somewhere on the walls of the container. Note that *ml* is equivalent to *cm³*, and *l* is to *dm³*. The mass can then be calculated. From *mass = density × volume*, a rearrangement from the density formula, we can find the mass by plugging in the density of water 1 *g/cm³* and the volume you've just got.

iii. When you add salt to the water, the volume is considered constant, as the salt dissolves in the water, whereas the mass increases slightly. Let the mass of the salt be . You can get:

$$1.05 = \frac{mass\ of\ water + x}{volume}$$

Rearrange, and you can get:

$$1.05 \times volume = mass\ of\ water + x$$
$$x = 1.05 \times volume - mass\ of\ water$$

Procedure:

1. Using the result from your calculation, add the right amount of salt to the water and stir.

2. Prepare fresh water and add one drop of food coloring to a glass of clean water. Stir until the color appears to be even throughout the water.

3. Use the dropper to slowly add the colored water to the top surface of the saltwater. Be careful with this step. We want to minimize the mixing of these two layers of water. Stop when the water level is around 2/3 of the height of the container.

4. Insert the board close to one end of the container. Add more colored water to the section of water separated by the board. The newly added water should be at least 2 cm high.

5. When you're ready, pull the board vertically, smoothly, and quickly. The most important part is to ensure the board leaves the water smoothly. Please don't go too fast; keeping the process smooth is more important.

6. Watch on the side of the container!

Influences of internal waves— Why are they so important?

One big question for the entire study of internal waves could be: Why are we studying them? This is an excellent question to ask when we talk about a new field of research or are introduced to an unfamiliar topic. What has motivated oceanographers for a long time is how meaningful internal waves are to nature and human beings, and there are so many reasons they are meaningful. In this section, we will approach this question by looking into five significant reasons.

1) Climate

In 2023, the Arctic experienced its sixth-warmest year since 1900. The sea ice in the Arctic has been melting by over 10% every decade, and it is also melting faster than ever. Global warming is indeed an urgent crisis that no one can neglect. The ocean circulation plays a highly significant role in global climate. It is suspected to be involved in the process of ice melting by passing heat to the Arctic. Globally, circulation works as the ocean carries warm water from the tropics to high-latitude regions and cold water the other way around. This circulation is called thermohaline circulation. "Thermo" means heat, and "haline" stands for salt. Inside the ocean, there is vertical transport of energy driven by internal waves, or so-called "**mixing**," as the waves interact and dissipate energy.

As internal waves propagate in the ocean, they carry energy. Their interactions with other waves, currents, and topography transfer energy. Among the interactions, wave-wave interactions are responsible for the most energy exchange. Waves with different parameters and sizes exchange energy, and small-scale waves gain lots as a result. As for topography, near the seafloor, internal waves are scattered off the topographic features, diminishing the scale of the waves. Finally, internal waves become very small and unsteady, generating turbulence. One way is by denser water at the wave crest moving over less dense water. Energy is taken away from the internal waves during the process. Turbulence shifts heat from the warmer water near the surface to water further down in the deep, cold ocean. In the open ocean, the turbulence can range from decimeters to hundreds of meters, lasting up to hours.

From the climate change perspective, it is essential to understand internal waves to develop good climate change models. While being one of the crucial ocean mechanisms affecting the climate, according to Ron Prinn, director of MIT's Center for the Science and Policy of Global Climate Change, the mixing due to breaking internal waves remains largely unrevealed, creating one of the most significant uncertainties in the models. Little progress has been made in the study of breaking internal waves. As described by Professor Raffaele Ferrari, it is "one of the outstanding problems" in learning how internal waves break, "we can probably account for 20 percent, but we can't account for the other 80 percent. It's a missing link."

Does ice melt faster in salt water or fresh water?
Make a prediction first. Then do a quick experiment to find out!

1. Drop a dyed ice cube into a glass of fresh water and a glass of salt water simultaneously.
2. Start the timer and record the time when the ice cube disappears.

Interestingly, ice melts faster in fresh water, although salt water has a lower freezing point. What mechanism makes fresh water the winner?

When ice melts in fresh water, the cold water sinks, causing the warmer water to always be in contact with the ice cube, which speeds up the melting process. However, in saltwater, the ice cube, despite being colder, cannot sink because the water below it is denser. As a result, the ice cube remains in contact with the colder fresh water, causing it to melt much more slowly.

2) Coral reef

Internal waves not only transfer heat. They also provide a channel for nutrition to be cycled in the ocean. They can carry cold and nutrient-rich water from the deeper ocean to shallow coastal areas, impacting water properties and affecting the metabolism of benthic communities in coastal ecosystems like kelp forests and coral reefs. Metabolism refers to all the chemical reactions inside cells that provide energy for the body. Every living organism depends on its surroundings for nutrients and materials necessary for movement, growth, reproduction, and survival.

Waters of the Australian North West Shelf, near Ningaloo Reef, are found to be nutrient-poor. However, the nutrients there are rapidly recycled on time scales of hours to days. Physical processes such as upwelling and internal waves have been identified as possible mechanisms for delivering nutrients from the deep offshore ocean to the surface, nearshore environment.

This is not the only evidence that internal waves benefit coral reefs. Oceanographers observed that internal waves reaching Dongsha Atoll cause a cooling effect on the near-surface waters of the east fore reef, lowering their temperature by 0.2°C during summer, and this influence of internal waves fluctuates both with tides and seasons. The water affected by internal waves on the fore reef is carried onto the shallow reef flat by tides and surface waves. This water can cool the reef by up to 2.0°C (with a variability of ±0.2°C), with an average cooling of 0.1 to 0.2°C during the study period. Additionally, it improves instantaneous nitrate fluxes by around four times. Therefore, internal waves generated over 500 kilometers away from Dongsha Island may have significantly influenced this shallow reef ecosystem's thermal stress and metabolism. For instance, a statistical model of bleaching factors by Dr Aryan Safaie and his colleagues suggests that without the cooling effect of internal waves on the Dongsha reef flat, the probability of severe bleaching would increase fourfold.

3) Submarine

As the dominating tool for acoustic signal transmission underwater, sonar is equipped by submarines to do a range of things, including but not limited to navigation, communication, and detection. There are two types of sonar: passive and active. The first refers to passively listening for sounds emitted by vessels, whereas the second means actively emitting sound pulses and detecting the echoes. Regardless of type, sound propagation is a necessary component. However, internal waves have a nonnegligible impact on ocean acoustic signal transmission. They induce fluctuations in sound propagation, posing challenges for submarine detection and negatively affecting the sonar system's performance.

Internal waves can be hazardous to submarines, not only by affecting their signal detections. Accidents caused by internal waves are recorded: for instance, in 1963, the nuclear submarine USS Thresher was lost with all hands onboard on its shakedown cruise. Before sinking, there had been no indication of unusual storm weather that could be responsible for this tragedy. Scientists suspect that the submarine probably dropped suddenly to greater depths as the craft slid down the back of the towering internal wave. This happens when the length of the submarine is comparable to the wave's wavelength.

As early as World War II, internal waves had this "bad reputation" of sinking submarines. Submarines purposely avoided the Strait of Gibraltar for how risky it could be to pass through. One reason was that internal waves propagated undersea. The threats posed by internal waves on submarines grabbed the attention of the U.S. Navy and the Soviet Navy. During the Cold War, in a report published by the U.S. Navy, sinkings of submarines caused by internal waves were described as "uncontrollable." Internal waves have been suspected to be the cause of numerous submarine incidents.

More facts

1. The German U-boats seriously threatened the Allies during World War Two. In his memoirs, *The Second World War, Volume 2*, Winston Churchill noted, "The only thing that ever really frightened me during the war was the U-boat peril."
2. HMS Oxley, the first submarine lost by Britain, was accidentally mistaken for a U-boat by HMS Triton, a friendly fire. The first actual U-boat was sunk four days later.

3. During the Battle of the Atlantic (1939-1943), the Allies developed various technologies to counter the threat of U-boats. One such technology was Asdic, a type of sonar initially created before the First World War. It was enhanced to enable better detection capabilities. Also, anti-submarine operations improved vastly during the battle. By 1943, all Atlantic convoys could be provided with air cover.

4) Offshore Drilling Platform

Apart from submarines, constructions in the ocean are threatened as well. Though not as destructive as tsunamis, large oceanic internal waves carry a considerable amount of energy, and the associated current flows can be strong enough to be a crucial factor considered in the design of offshore drilling platforms and other similar structures. Offshore drilling platforms are structures equipped with facilities and supplies to drill an oil well in the sea.

Constructions in the ocean, such as offshore drilling platforms, are affected by strong shear currents induced by internal waves in that the shear currents twist the cables and poles and sometimes damage them. In an incident in the Northern Andaman Sea, a marginal sea of the northeastern Indian Ocean, a rig tilted by 3 degrees when an internal passed through. This caused a 2-meter increase in the draft on one of the legs of the structure and nearly a 25% increase in anchor tension on one side of the rig. Draft is the distance between the bottom of the structure and the waterline, i.e., the water level.

When impacted by internal waves, the construction may require expensive repair, further increasing the financial loss by reducing the work time. Even occasionally, workers' safety might be affected. One example is Alexander Kielland Platform in the North Sea, which collapsed in 1980, resulting in the deaths of 123 people. After the accident, people discovered that one of the poles had flaws. Therefore, studying internal waves to develop a well-designed early warning system is very important.

Experiment to see how constructions are affected!

1. Set up the experiment as in section 3, steps 1-5.
2. Make a paper craft, which will be your model of the construction (e.g., an offshore drilling platform). A paper boat might be the easiest, but you can also make one as complicated as a drilling platform.
3. Cover the surface with waterproof tape. Attach a string the length of the water level to the bottom of your model—tape is still your best choice. Tie a bracelet bead or any other small object that has sufficient weight. You will see what this means in the next step!
4. Place the model on the surface of the water. The object needs to sink to the bottom of the container, and the weight you attached should keep the string straight.
5. Generate an internal wave as in section step 6, and observe how the string and the papercraft respond to the wave!

5) In the Atmosphere

In the atmosphere, airplanes experience internal waves, too. As oceanic internal waves stand for waves within the ocean, internal waves in the atmosphere exist between air layers of different densities. However, note that internal waves in the atmosphere have unique names. In the atmosphere, internal waves can be generated by thunderstorms or by air flowing over a mountain range. The second type of internal wave is called "mountain waves."

Internal waves in the atmosphere could impose dangers on airplanes. According to a report by MIT professor Thomas Peacock in 2008, when an Air Canada plane was cruising from Victoria to Toronto under clear skies, neither the pilots nor the air traffic controllers detected any severe weather on their radar screens. However, suddenly and unexpectedly, the plane plunged 2,000 feet in just 15 seconds, followed by another 2,000 feet descent, before the pilot regained control and stabilized the aircraft. Ten people suffered injuries that needed hospital treatment. Later, scientists revealed that the cause of the plunge was a mountain wave on the Lee side, the side of a mountain range sheltered from the wind, of the Rockies Mountains in North America.

Do not worry, though. Such accidents rarely happen. Pilots will avoid the area influenced by mountain waves when designing the flight route. Although the images would not be sufficient for pilots to find out the altitude of the turbulence, satellites can help identify clues of mountain waves. Also, past pilot reports can provide helpful information for future pilots to check whether their intended routes are safe. Still, internal waves add complexity to flights over certain places and at specific times of the year.

The Morning Glory

From late September to early November, gliders travel from all over the world to Burketown, Australia to surf the Morning Glory, a rare meteorological phenomenon happening this time of the year—a type of roll cloud, or arcus cloud, that can stretch up to 1,000 kilometers in length and reach heights of 1 to 2 kilometers, typically hovering just 100 to 200 meters above the ground. Royal Australian Air Force pilots first reported it as a type of internal wave in 1942.

Burketown is the only place where Morning Glory forms regularly. It forms in the Gulf of Carpentaria due to specific atmospheric conditions. During the day, sea breezes from the east and west converge over the Cape York peninsula, causing air to rise and form clouds. A stable layer forms over the gulf at night due to a surface inversion. Descending air from the peninsula generates rolling cylinders across the gulf, creating waves where air rises at the front and sinks at the rear. In the early morning, saturated air at the front produces a cloud that becomes the leading edge of the Morning Glory cloud. This cloud evaporates at the back of the cylinder, contributing to the formation of the phenomenon.

When you see a morning glory visiting Burketown, "It's quite an eerie sensation as the wind picks up and the temperature drops," said Amanda Wilkinson, Burketown's Savannah Lodge owner and town resident for 30 years. "And then it's amazing. You get some whoppers with smooth, cylindrical clouds and others with fluffy bits at the top. When you get a nice big one, it's unbelievable." She noted that when the clouds pass over the town, it feels as if you could almost reach up and touch them. According to a glider, "You just feel tiny, and you feel the true majesty of nature."

How Do Oceanographers Study Internal Waves? And What Are Some of Their Findings?

It's hard to say whether internal waves are our friends or enemies. They are contradictorily helpful and destructive. This is quite common, just like the two sides of a coin. People study them to learn both how to use their benefits and ways to avoid their harms.

The scientists are conducting field research, which involves collecting data outside the laboratory, library, or workplace. In other words, they are collecting data in nature rather than in a lab. Other kinds of research include ocean observations, lab research, theoretical studies, and numerical modelling. This section will discuss these research methods in more detail.

1) Methods of Research

Observations

Remote Sensing

There are mainly two ways to collect data on true internal waves in real life: remote sensing and field research. We will explore remote sensing first. To start with, we must introduce a type of internal wave mentioned earlier: internal solitary waves. Although they are below the water's surface, they can often be seen from above.

Internal solitary waves are a special kind of internal wave with a single crest. They can preserve their waveform over a long distance due to the balance of two essential factors—nonlinearity and non-hydrostatic dispersion. Nonhydrostatic dispersion is the effect that tends to spread out the internal wave, whereas nonlinearity tends to steepen the wave. When the two effects are balanced, the waveform is preserved while traveling a long distance.

Recall that when there is an internal solitary wave inside the ocean, it induces currents inside, thus forming convergence and divergence. For example, if the wave travels towards you, you will see the convergence zone first, in which the internal wave causes a downwelling of water and a rough water surface. Then, you will see water upwelling in the divergence zone after the convergence, so the water surface will smooth in this area. The front of a wave is dark, and the back is bright to human eyes, while to one of the most commonly used SAR (Synthetic Aperture Radar) satellites, the bright and dark bands are opposite to human eyes, i.e., the front is bright, and the back is dark.

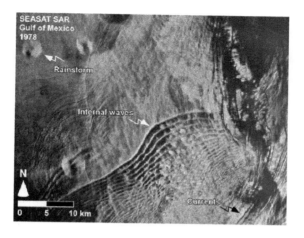

Figure of the SAR image of internal waves, with convergence and divergence labeled

Oceanographers take photos of the area in the ocean they are interested in via satellites from above. Examining the surface, they can obtain parameters of the internal waves captured, such as the direction of propagation, half-width, number of waves, the distance between neighboring waves, and wave speed. Remote sensing is a helpful tool for field research, as it can collect information over a long distance but still of high resolution. Yet, they face limitations when it comes to continuously observing the same wave packet over time or tracking the evolution of specific wave interactions. As a result, SAR imaging is less suitable for research requiring analysis at small spatial and temporal scales. To overcome these challenges, airplane remote sensing is proposed, as it grants scientists more control over the spatial and temporal scale. Small airplanes such as float airplane and Unmanned Aerial Vehicle (UAV) are popular options.

For more about SAR Satellites, look at page 56!

Field Research

As mentioned, field research and remote sensing are two ways to observe internal waves in real life. Remote sensing takes indirect measurements, whereas field research takes direct measurements. The most common way is by sending equipment down into the ocean water. Then there are two choices for oceanographers: 1. When the ship that carries the equipment arrives at the target area in the ocean, the equipment is lowered into the ocean while still attached to the ship by ropes. The equipment travels within the water body at the desired depth as the ship sails over the ocean surface. 2. While the equipment dives into the ocean, the ship leaves the area to complete its next mission or return to the harbor. The equipment will be recovered after some time, so information at this fixed position will be collected. Either way, measurements of temperature, salinity, and current field can be obtained.

Standard equipments used by oceanographers include Acoustic Doppler Current Profiler and current meter. It measures current velocities by using sound waves that bounce off particles in the water. Another example is CTD, which stands for conductivity, temperature, and depth. It gathers information on seawater's electrical conductivity, temperature, and pressure. The first is to determine salinity, whereas the last can give the depth of the equipment.

Laboratory Study

The earliest lab was set up by Greek scientist and philosopher Pythagoras of Samos (c. 570 – c. 495 BC), who experimented on tones and strings. As you can imagine, it was not a proper lab like the one in schools and institutions today. Pythagoras carried out this experiment at his home, and this was the origin of labs. From this point of view, a lab is basically where experiments are performed.

In modern days, a lab usually has lots of apparatus for people to do more complicated research. For physical oceanographers, a lab is a place where they can simulate ocean conditions. Scientists studying internal waves often set up experiments using the method introduced in section 3 or similar ones. There are many things to study. For example, some people are interested in how an internal wave is influenced by seafloor topography, so they might produce an internal wave in a water tank with a specific type of topography set at the bottom and observe how the wave behaves differently. Some people are interested in the interaction between waves. They may produce two internal waves, so let them meet and see what happens. You have generated an internal wave in Section 3 and tested how ice melting is affected by salinity. We will look into more experiments on internal waves in part 2.

Theoretical Study

When we talk about theories of internal waves, we usually mean equations that we can solve straightforwardly without using numerical modeling. There is more than one equation for internal waves, yet identifying which is more suitable for the wave you are investigating must be done before further calculations.

To study internal waves, wave amplitude is a significant factor in determining the type of internal wave and, thus, how oceanographers should approach the study. Internal waves can be divided into linear and nonlinear according to their amplitudes. Linear internal waves are waves with very small amplitudes and can be described by linear theory. Nonlinear internal waves, on the other hand, are waves with large enough amplitudes that nonlinear effects have become important. As their name has shown, they can only be described by nonlinear theory, and their propagation speeds are always larger than what linear theory predicts.

With this knowledge, we can examine how theories fall into these categories. For linear internal waves with very, very small amplitudes, linear equations can solve the problem. When the amplitudes of the waves are relatively larger but not very large, weakly nonlinear equations are used. Examples of these weakly nonlinear equations include the Korteweg–De Vries equation and the Benjamin-Ono equation, which will be introduced later in this section (page 50). We need to use fully nonlinear equations when we come to strongly nonlinear waves with large amplitudes. However, fully nonlinear equations cannot be solved with analytical solutions. This is when numerical modeling comes in, which is finding approximate solutions using computers.

Research Methods

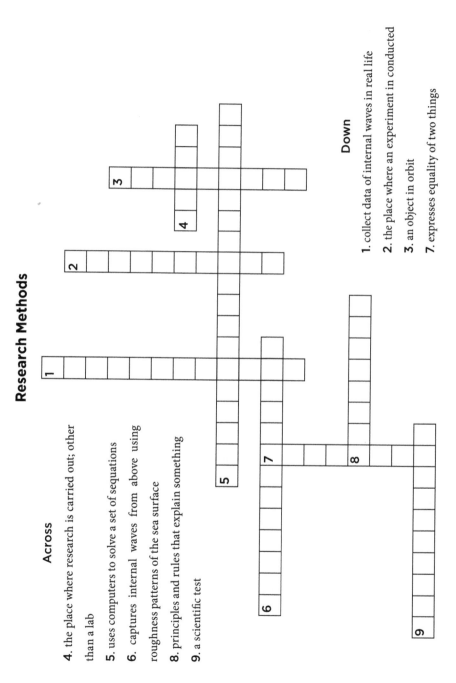

Across

4. the place where research is carried out; other than a lab

5. uses computers to solve a set of sequations

6. captures internal waves from above using roughness patterns of the sea surface

8. principles and rules that explain something

9. a scientific test

Down

1. collect data of internal waves in real life

2. the place where an experiment in conducted

3. an object in orbit

7. expresses equality of two things

2) Some interesting findings

Ekman's research on the dead-water phenomenon

After his expedition, Nansen became very interested in the dead-water phenomenon, and he found physicist and meteorologist (a scientist who studies weather) Vilhelm Bjerknes to study this mystery. Bjerknes did not investigate the phenomenon on his own. Instead, he asked his student Vagn Walfrid Ekman to do that for him. Ekman, therefore, became the first person to study internal waves in a lab.

Ekman set up two layers of water in a water tank. As we did in section 3, the bottom layer was denser than the top freshwater layer. A slight difference is that he dyed the bottom layer rather than the top. Still, the purpose was the same: for easy interface identification, and thus, the internal wave that was generated. A model of the ship, Fram, was made and attached to a rope, which Ekman later pulled. As shown in the picture, internal waves were generated as a result. They interacted with the ship and produced a drag, causing abnormality in the ship's movement.

Later, people learned more about this phenomenon. To summarize, when internal waves sway a ship back and forth, two drag phenomena can result. The first is called Nansen wave-making drag, which leads to persistent but plodding progress on the boat, as Nansen experienced. The second is called Ekman wave-making drag. As the name suggests, Ekman observed it. It causes speed fluctuations in the affected vessel.

Redo Ekman's experiment!

Set up the experiment as in section 3, steps 1–3. Make a paper boat and wrap it with waterproof tape. Use tape to attach a string to the bow of the ship. Place the boat gently on the water surface, close to one end of the tank, with the bow facing the other. Pull the string with a constant force. Observe the effects of internal waves!

More about the dead-water phenomenon: behind the Battle of Actium (31 BC)

The Battle of Actium occurred on the Ionian Sea, near the Roman spot of Actium in Greece. In the Battle, Roman General Marc Antony and the Egyptian Pharaoh, Cleopatra VII joined forces to fight against Roman military leader Octavian's fleet. However, they lost the battle, and Octavian emerged as the dominant figure in Rome. Eventually, he became known as "Augustus Caesar" and "the First Citizen" of Rome.

Cleopatra   Octavian   Antony

Legend says that the defeat was due to remoras, or 'suckerfish', attached to the hulls of the fleet. However, some scientists suspect the Egyptian fleet may have encountered the dead-water phenomenon during the battle, slowing them down. It is possible, as the place where the battle happened, the Bay of Actium had fjord-like features—remember that fjords are suitable locations for internal waves to form!

Modern scientists and mathematicians at the CNRS' Institut Pprime and the Laboratoire de Mathématiques et Applications (CNRS/Université de Poitiers) investigated this possibility in a major project on the reasons why Cleopatra's large ships lost when they faced Octavian's weaker vessels. Their study involves a mathematical classification of different internal waves and an analysis of experimental images at the sub-pixel scale for the first time. They found out that the speed variations of the dead-water phenomenon are because of the formation of certain waves on which the ship moves back and forth as if it's on "an undulating conveyor belt." Also, they discovered that the speed fluctuations are temporary. The boat will eventually return to the slow but constant speed experienced by Nansen.

More facts

1. Cleopatra and Antony committed suicide a year after the battle. Cleopatra's son Caesarion became the next Pharaoh. Caesarion's rule over Egypt was short-lived. Octavian swiftly conquered Egypt, declaring it a Roman province. Tragically, Caesarion's life was cut short at the tender age of 17. He met his end on August 23, 30 BC, marking the conclusion of his brief and tumultuous reign.

2. Octavian, or Augustus, never formally claimed the title of Emperor for himself. He liked "First Citizen" more. But he named a month after himself—August.

Internal Wave Spectrum

The study of internal waves did not grow rapidly throughout the journey after pioneering research from people like Nansen and Ekman. The outbreak of World War II and technical obstacles slowed it down. Nevertheless, in the 1940s, breakthroughs in research instruments brought life back to the field and enabled lots of development in the next few decades. During this period of quick advancements, theories and research methods improved largely. The internal wave spectrum is an excellent example of this.

Observations of the internal wave spectrum in the ocean reveal a remarkable consistency in its shape across deep ocean regions unless observed near a significant source of internal waves. When we observe the sea surface, we see waves that aren't simple sinusoids. Instead, there are random waves with different lengths and periods. Describing this surface accurately is more complex. However, by simplifying it, we can approach a description of it. These simplifications give rise to the concept of the spectrum of ocean waves. A wave spectrum describes how wave energy is distributed across different frequencies and wavelengths.

Christopher Garrett and Walter Munk (1972) initially proposed an analytical form approximating the internal wave spectrum, later refining it in 1975 (Garrett and Munk, 1975). Consolidating numerous observations into a single, straightforward formula was a milestone that changed the research direction. As Munk pointed out, learning the sources, sinks, evolution, and interactions of internal waves is now more critical.

Walter Munk

Walter Munk is a distinguished American physical oceanographer. His early research on quantitatively predicting surf conditions played a vital role in the success of Allied amphibious landings during World War II. He was among the first few scientists to introduce statistical methods to oceanographic data analysis. He led the field of oceanography, and his groundbreaking work earned him prestigious awards such as the National Medal of Science and the Kyoto Prize, along with induction into the French Legion of Honour. Some people called him the "Einstein of oceanography"!

You might not have expected how he found his interest in oceanography: When he was young, his grades suffered because he spent too much time skiing. His family then sent him from Austria to a boys' preparatory school in upper New York State. They hoped he would pursue a career in finance, so they let him work at the family's banking firm. But Munk didn't enjoy banking at all. He left the firm and attended the California Institute of Technology—perhaps thought that it would be more fun. It turned out that he found his real interest there and stepped on a jouney for his whole life—until he passed away, aged 101.

MIT General Circulation Model and Navier-Stokes equations

Also known as MITgcm, the MIT General Circulation Model is a numerical model that can be used to study the atmosphere and the ocean and address small-scale and large-scale phenomena. This model is based on the Navier-Stokes equations, which describe the flow of incompressible fluids derived by Claude-Louis Navier and George Gabriel Stokes.

Navier-Stokes equations root in Newton's Second Law. When there is a resultant force acting on an object, a fluid in this case, this force is equal to the product of the mass of the object and the acceleration of the object (the rate of change of velocity), or sometimes people use another interpretation: the rate of change in momentum with time. The momentum of an object is the product of its mass and velocity. Apart from Newton's Second Law, viscosity is another term that needs to be introduced here. Viscosity is a measure of how a fluid is resistant to flow. Honey is more viscous than oil, and oil is more viscous than water. Before the equations were introduced, Euler's equations were used to describe the inviscid flow of fluids. The Navier-Stokes equations first took into account viscosity, making them more realistic.

Navier-Stokes equations are the foundation of the entire theoretical study of oceanography. They cannot be solved exactly—at least mathematicians haven't found an exact solution today—but with assumptions made. MIT-gcm is a numerical computer code that solves the equations based on the Boussinesq assumption. It is an invaluable tool to study non-hydrostatic dynamics, such as internal waves with complicated topography, including canyons and ridges in the ocean. This advantage makes it one of oceanographers' most popular numerical models.

Isaac Newton	Claude-Louis Navier	Sir George Stokes
1642–1727	1785–1836	1819–1903

The Millennium Prize Problems

In 2000, the Clay Institute of Cambridge, Massachusetts, announced prize problems to celebrate the millennium. They are seven of the most challenging unsolved math problems at that time. Anyone who presents a correct solution will receive 1 million from the Scientific Advisory Board of the Institute. The Navier-Stokes equations appeared to be among the questions. Still unanswered today, the problem is as below:

$$\nabla \cdot \overline{u} = 0$$

$$\rho \frac{D\overline{u}}{Dt} = -\nabla p + \mu \nabla^2 \overline{u} + \rho \overline{F}$$

This is the equation which governs the flow of fluids such as water and air. However, there is no proof for the most basic questions one can ask: "Do solutions exist, and are they unique? Why ask for a proof? Because a proof gives not only certitude, but also understanding."

KdV and BO Equations

The KdV equation stands for the weakly non-linear Korteweg–De Vries equation. Initially proposed by Boussinesq in 1877, the concept was later rediscovered by Diederik Korteweg and Gustav de Vries 1895, who experimented with long one-dimensional waves at a certain depth in a shallow water channel. It is a model that describes internal waves with long wavelengths but small amplitudes in the ocean where density stratification occurs. It is also applicable to describing weakly nonlinear shallow-water waves and a few kinds of acoustic waves. The KdV equation has helped oceanographers find internal wave parameters for many years.

Brooke Benjamin derived the BO equation in 1967, and Hiroaki Ono later in 1975. Named after them, this weakly nonlinear equation, Benjamin-Ono equation, describes the one-dimensional, one-way propagation of long weakly nonlinear internal waves in deep water with a specific type of stratification—between two layers of different densities, a region with continuous density variation exists.

Both the KdV and the BO Equations are only applicable to solitary waves. In the field of internal waves, they mean internal solitary waves. In fact, there are solitary surface waves as well. The two equations help oceanographers in similar ways. They give solutions to the wave speed and expressions of the amplitude. From these, oceanographers can find the speed of an internal wave if they have the amplitude in hand and the amplitude if they have the wave speed in hand. The difference between the two equations is the conditions for them to be applicable. The KdV equation works for internal waves in shallow water, which is defined as water with a depth smaller than the horizontal dimension of the internal wave. The horizontal dimension of an internal solitary wave is the half-width of the wave. The BO equation is suitable for internal waves in deep water, which is the opposite of shallow water.

Internal solitary waves in real life

Strictly speaking, waves theoretically described as internal solitary waves do not exist in real life. Many factors influence the wave but are not considered by the theories. For example, energy dissipation (loss of energy), background currents, changes in stratification, etc., are all not taken into account. As often in science, theory tends to be more ideal, based on assumptions and simplifications, while reality is more complicated. So-called "internal solitary" waves are actually internal "solitary-like" waves.

Wave-wave Interaction

According to John Miles:

Wave-wave interaction occurs when waves interact with each other. When two waves with finite amplitudes intersect, they can influence each other. This differs from linear waves, which simply superimpose without mutual impact. In 1977, John Miles proposed a set of methods to classify the interactions between solitary internal waves, a few ways to group interactions, and the groups are called the following: "strong" and "weak," "symmetric" and "asymmetric," "regular" and "Mach," and "phase-conserving" and "phase-not-conserving."

"Strong" and "weak" are distinguished according to the time duration of the interaction and the magnitude of the impact on the waves. When two waves travel in nearly the same direction, strong interaction occurs as the time length of interaction is rather long, and the impact is significant. On the other hand, when two waves propagate in entirely different directions, the interaction happens quickly and has minor effects on the waves. This interaction is considered to be weak.

The "symmetric" and "asymmetric" classification is applied using a different rule, the interaction angle and wave amplitude difference. The interaction angle is the angle between the normals (the imaginary line perpendicular to the wavefront, showing the propagation direction of the wave) of the two interacting waves. To use this classification, the sizes of the wave amplitude difference and the interaction angle are compared. The interaction angle exceeding the amplitude difference indicates "symmetry," and the opposite leads to "asymmetry." This is because when the difference between the amplitudes of two interacting waves is slight, the interaction can be taken as a reflection, one of the waves being treated as the incident wave and the other as the image. Just like the reflection of light, incident and reflected rays create symmetry!

Now we come to "Mach" and "regular." "Mach" is a singular case different from "regular," which is the more common wave interaction according to this classification method. When two waves meet at a small interaction angle under specific conditions of wave amplitude, Mach interaction occurs instead of regular. This leads to the genaration of a third wave, known as the Mach stem. Interestingly, this extra wave appears perpendicular to the original waves' path, away from where they met. Over time, the length of the wavefront of this Mach stem grows longer, making the interaction dynamic instead of steady. Mach interaction is a mechanism for generating waves with much larger amplitude, suggesting stronger currents. These enormous waves might even cause breaking, which can enhance mixing. Additionally, there's a chance for energy to transfer between different waveforms in this process. Essentially, Mach interaction reveals the complex dance of waves.

The last classification separates interactions into "phase-conserving" and "phase-not-conserving" groups. It requires using some formulas and calculations to put wave-wave interactions into the correct categories. They are also essential, but the groupings are more complicated.

According to the interaction angle:
Wave interaction patterns can also be categorized into seven types, as in the cartoons. What determines the type of wave interaction, in this case, is the interaction angle. When waves travel in the same direction—indicating zero interaction angle—but the rear wave is faster and catches up (case 1), the front wave shifts backward while the rear one shifts forward. Here, the occasion that the front wave is faster is not considered because there won't be any interaction.

(1) 0° interaction angle (Overtaking)
large wave shifts forward, small wave shifts backward

Then, we come to the cases where there are non-zero interaction angles. At small interaction angles (case 2), one wave moves forward while the other moves backward.

(2) small interaction angle
one wave shifts forward, one wave shifts backward

You'll probably find yourself quite familiar with case 3. Indeed, it is exactly the same as the Mach interaction, and a Mach stem is produced as a result.

(3) small interaction angle (Mach interaction)
outgoing waves change propagation direction

For medium angles, which are angles less than 120° but much greater than 0° (case 4), both waves shift forward.

(4) medium interaction angle
both waves shift forward

The turning point is at the interaction angle of 120° (case 5). In this scenario, neither wave experiences a change.

(5) 120° interaction angle
nothing changes

At angles between 120° and 180° (case 6), both waves shift backward.

(6) large interaction angle
both waves shift backward

Finally, when waves approach each other from precisely opposite directions (case 7), creating a 180° interaction angle, it is called a "head-on collision." Still, both waves shift backward.

(7) 180° interaction angle (head-on collision)
both waves shift backward

SAR Satellite

SAR satellite is one of oceanographers' most common remote sensing observation methods. SAR stands for Synthetic Aperture Radar. Aperture is a word commonly used in photography. It is the opening of a camera that allows light to pass through. It can be adjusted to control the amount of light entering the camera. However, it is different when we talk about Synthetic Aperture Radar. Unlike cameras, which capture existing light, the sensors emit radiation and collect the returned information. The radiation they emit is microwaves, which have smaller frequencies and longer wavelengths than visible light. The aperture is the part of the antenna that carries out this work.

The clarity of radar data is tied to the ratio of the sensor's wavelength to the antenna's length. Simply put, longer antennas produce better spatial resolution for a given wavelength. Unfortunately, a massive antenna isn't feasible for a satellite sensor in space. To overcome this limitation, scientists and engineers developed a clever solution: synthetic aperture. This technique involves combining data from multiple acquisitions using a shorter antenna to mimic the effect of a larger antenna, thus enhancing the resolution of the data collected.

SAR satellites are useful tools for oceanographers to perform remote sensing. They can work all day long, regardless of many kinds of weather conditions, making them one of the most important sensors for internal wave observations. A few famous SAR satellites include the European Remote Sensing Satellites (ERS) 1 and 2 and the Canadian RADARSAT.

ERS-2

RADARSAT

Quiz time! Test how much you know about satellites . . .

1. What is the minimum velocity for a satellite to stay in orbit?
   A. 1,200 km/h
   B. 9,600 km/h
   C. 28,000 km/h
   D. 71,000 km/h

2. Which of the following is the Earth's first artificial satellite?
   A. Vanguard 1
   B. Sputnik-1
   C. Explorer 1
   D. Bhaskara I

3. Which of the following is a natural satellite?
   A. The Moon
   B. Neptune
   C. Halley's Comet
   D. Mansonia

Answers:

1. C.

2. B. Vanguard 1 is the first satellite to have solar electric power. Explorer 1 is the first satellite launched by the United States. Bhaskara I was the first experimental remote-sensing satellite.

3. A. A natural satellite is an astronomical object that orbits a planet, dwarf planet, or small Solar System body. Neptune is a planet that orbits the Sun, classified as a star. Halley's comet also orbits the Sun. Mansonia is a kind of mosquito.

From the Seafloor: Volcano Eruption

Have you ever thought of volcano eruptions underwater as a source of internal waves? Recall that the most common sources of internal waves are wind, tide, currents, etc. How can a volcano eruption generate internal waves in the ocean?

This is an infrequent occasion, first observed when the Tongan volcano, Hunga Tonga-Hunga Ha'apai volcano, erupted in the southwest of the Pacific Ocean in 2022. SAR images captured by the European Space Agency's Sentinel-1 revealed the propagation of internal waves in the northern area where the eruption occurred. There was no sign of internal waves in this area 12 days before and after the eruption, according to the Sentinel-1's observation. The generation of internal waves needs two factors: stratification and disturbance, and steady stratification is already known to be presented in this part of the Pacific Ocean. How did disturbance come, then?

Oceanographers suggest the collapse of heavy seawater to be the cause. When the volcano erupts, the heavy seawater deep in the ocean is blown upwards and flows near the volcano. Because it is denser than other water at this depth, it sinks after the eruption, disturbing the stratification. The magma from the volcano carries a large amount of thermal energy, which is then transferred to the seawater nearby as kinetic energy, the energy of motion. As the kinetic energy spreads around, the disturbance is magnified. The disturbance will eventually become internal waves when meeting other volcanos in this area (there are many volcanoes around the edges of the Pacific Ocean). The stratification in this area could be more robust. The disturbance must be vigorous enough to compensate for internal waves to be produced.

It is unlikely that this is the first time volcano eruptions have caused internal waves to form, but this is indeed the first time people have observed that. There are a few reasons that may have contributed to this result. A few satellites are in orbit, yet revisiting the exact location takes a long time. Cloud cover often obscures the satellites, making them less reliable for continuous monitoring. Lastly, internal waves have small-scale features that are challenging to detect accurately from space.

Internal waves in the atmosphere

Volcano eruptions are sometimes responsible for generating internal waves in the atmosphere. Observations from Montserrat, a Caribbean Island, reveal that incredibly explosive volcanic eruptions can create internal waves in the atmosphere. These waves are detectable by microbarographs at ground level. Scientists suggest that if they could be interpreted, monitoring them can provide early indications of volcanic activity, especially when other methods are impractical due to factors like bad weather, poor visibility, or remote locations.

To the Surface: Sea Ice

Polar areas are like sentinels of the climate crisis. They are very sensitive and respond quickly to changes. Internal waves play an important part in sea ice evolution in the polar areas. They have been found responsible for some flexure of sea ice and the formation of ice bands, and they impact sea traffic, fisheries, offshore operations, and military marine activities. Therefore, they interest oceanographers very much.

Unfortunately, for this direction of study, field research has the disadvantage of the inability to perform a fair test for one variable (i.e., scientists cannot examine the effects of just one individual factor), as well as the hazard arising from the severe conditions. Also, remote sensing via SAR satellites cannot observe all areas under weather conditions. As a result, the first internal wave and sea ice interaction experiment was carried out by Magda Carr et al. (et al. stands for "and others")

A similar setup as in section 3 was used for the experiment. But there was one change made: the water wasn't dyed. Instead, tiny light-reflective particles were added to the water. A light source was set up at the bottom of the container, which was a water tank as in a usual lab experiment setup. The particles would reflect the light, enabling a camera facing the water tank to record their movements. This beneficial and popular technique called Particle Image Velocimetry (PIV) allows scientists to analyze the flow field, i.e., the distribution of the density and velocity of the water, with the help of computer software such as DigiFlow or MATLAB. A piece of ice they were interested in was placed on the surface of the water. Then, the scientists generated an internal wave and observed how the ice was influenced by the wave and how the ice changed the wave.

The wave-ice interaction analysis covered many aspects, including the motion of the ice, the amplitude and shape of the wave, and energy dissipation under the ice. Like other lab research, calculations were conducted, and software was used to investigate the information collected and present the results. The results confirmed some theoretical studies and showed that the interaction between internal waves and sea ice may affect wave energy dissipation and, therefore, mixing in the polar oceans.

To recall details about mixing, go back to page 27!

I hope you have enjoyed this journey to discover internal waves. You can now tell your friends all you've learned and impress them—even adults! Next time you go to the beach, when you see the dynamic surface waves, remember that there might be "quiet" internal waves hiding below the ocean surface—or are they actually that quiet? No matter what, at times, people have not noticed them; they have accompanied us all the time.

About the Author

Jin Tan is a young oceanographer who has always been fascinated by internal waves. Loving the science of internal waves, she is now adventuring the interaction between sea ice and those beautiful waves. She is also exploring the ocean and other waters by sailing, photographing, and podcasting. Last but not least, she invites curious minds to join this thrilling expedition with her!